Christmas Memories

by A. C. Greene

Illustrations by Geoffrey Greene

University of North Texas Press

Denton, Texas

5 4 3 2 1

Requests for permission to reproduce material from this work
should be sent to:

Permissions
University of North Texas Press
P.O. Box 13856
Denton, TX 76203

The paper in this book meets the minimum requirements of the
American National Standard for Permanence of paper for
Printed Library Materials, Z39.48.1984.

Library of Congress Cataloging-in-Publication Data

Greene, A. C., 1923–
    Christmas memories / by A. C. Greene ; illustrations by
Geoffrey Greene.
            p.   cm.
    ISBN 1-57441-017-2 (alk. paper)
    1. Christmas—Texas. 2. Greene, A. C., 1923–   .
3. Texas—Biography. I. Title.
GT4986.T4G72   1996
394.2'663'09764—dc20   96-8410
                                                          CIP

The Too-Big Christmas Tree

Somewhere in your early years you begin to form your idea of Christmas. Not what it means as a religious festival, but the shape it should take to be the perfect season: the carols, the candles, the bells . . . angels, weathers, chimney-smoke at night, the hills of Bethlehem . . . all of that. And later, the regrets and sadnesses you cannot (and would not) shut out: the gifts you never gave and the gift you never got; sleigh rides you never took over snow that never fell; a sudden voice, so long gone it has no connection with time any more, only with Christmas.

Your idea of Christmas is usually like your idea of life: hopeful and glittery, lovely perhaps—and never quite achieved. But you accept the improbability of a perfect Christmas without denying your idea. Bethlehem gets farther, candles are dangerous, angels grow up—but Christmas keeps its shape. And although you never experience it the way you vision, the mold persists, and you hold to it, even if you have lost the star. There is a wholeness to the Christmas sights and sounds; the sensations, the tastes . . . and the smell.

A smell is hard to describe. The most satisfactory description is often an example: a baby smells "like" milk, a perfume smells "like" your wife. Smell is the most deeply personal of the senses because it involves the actual taking-in of an outside substance: into the nose, the head, the lungs. Taste, while similar in this respect, can be controlled. You may refuse to taste. But smell, often as not, is involuntary: it has penetrated without your having prepared for it. If it is powerful enough, charged strongly with emotion or memory, then you are thrust immediately into the world which one whiff has created, or brought back. That is the way the smell of

Christmas happens to me; it invades my being and becomes . . . "Christmas." And to me, Christmas smells like a cedar tree.

*T*here are many kinds of evergreens which are referred to as cedars. They share such characteristics as bushiness, pungent odor, and sharp, waxy needles. The green colors range from dusty gray to near emerald. What I grew up calling cedar is actually the Mexican juniper, a dark green shrub, heavy with fragrance, and bearing small, hard, purplish berries which (I discovered well after becoming an adult) give an identifying flavor to London gin.

In the drier part of Texas, where I originated, these cedars live successfully on thin soil where even the mesquite cannot thrive. Ranchers consider cedars to be not just a nuisance but a positive menace. The cedars suck up water from the grasses, they start erosion by destroying all vegetation under their low boughs, and they proliferate almost beyond human control if left uncut for a few years. Of the main floral pests of the grazing country—mesquite, prickly pear, and cedar—the cedar is held to be the worst. The mesquite drops an edible bean, and the fruit of the prickly pear can have its prickles burned off and be eaten by cattle, while the cedar in that part of Texas seldom grows straight or abundant enough to cut and market even for fence posts.

But it makes an admirable Christmas tree if one can overlook some of its natural imperfections, or accept them as marks of strength and adaptability. What is more nostalgic, to a believer in the Christmas smell, than a cedar close and warm inside the house in that season? How it guides the senses and shapes the memory. The cedar smell means more to me than any particular of Christmas except the music, and it may transcend that, in reality, because my ideal in Christmas music is the sound of carols coming across moonlighted snow, and where I have lived most of my life we seldom see snow at Christmastime. One year, when I was ten or eleven years old, someone in the family idly lighted a twig of cedar and, as the needles ignited then died to a smoking ember, remarked he wished the whole house could smell as good. My grandmother and I got a pan from the kitchen and took a smoldering branch throughout the house, making it cedar-fragrant everywhere. This became a tradition, and when I married and had children, we continued it. Christmas Eve we would sit before an open fire and sing carols, then take our smoking cedar from room to room, carrying the Christmas smell

to every corner, continuing our songs as
we went. Our problem today would be
that few cedars are available for Christmas
trees in the big cities. Nearly everyone uses
the pine and spruce imports. This is true to
a great extent even in the cedar country. I
suppose it's a matter of convenience, and I
will admit, these imports are more civilized
and amenable: they stand pretty and
regular, allowing the strings of lights to be
draped around them, just so. And too, they
contain so much moisture—coming from
the snowy climes, I guess—they are sup-
posed to be safer from fire. All this may be
true, but they have almost no fragrance
and, like a department store Santa Claus,

show that they are merely hired for the job.

When I was a boy in West Texas, nearly everyone used a cedar for a Christmas tree. Few fir, pine, or spruce trees were shipped in and most families, even wealthy ones, would have choked at the notion of paying good money for a tree. Going to the country to cut the Christmas tree was an important part of the seasonal ritual and, in retrospect, seems to have been almost as exciting as the gift-giving ceremony itself. Most families cut their Christmas cedar tree from ten days to two weeks before Christmas. If you cut a cedar much earlier than that, it had become a housekeeping hazard by the time it served its purpose, casting its needles everywhere in a shower of dry, brittle fall-out. After the manner of most children, I always wanted to keep the Christmas tree up and decorated much longer than the womenfolks would allow it—I might have acceded to its coming down by Valentine's Day—but New Year's Day was ordinarily the extreme limit of both the tree's and my mother's endurance.

In the town where I was born and raised, everyone drove a few miles south to cut a tree. Here a line of hills crossed the county east and west and the slopes were covered with cedars—in fact, one prominent area of those hills was named Cedar Gap. Even though hundreds of families came out to the hills to get trees, I never recall the landowners trying to charge a fee for cutting. I suppose they were happy enough to get rid of a few dozen of the pests. Of course, there was no market for them anyway. If you had brought a load of cedars into town to sell you would have been laughed off the streets. Cedars belong to everybody, was the community attitude, and half the fun of having a Christmas tree was going out to cut it.

With my family the tree cutting expedition always took place on a Sunday afternoon (after we had been to Sunday school and church services, understand). Looking for a tree, you didn't just motor directly out to some preselected spot and start felling. No, finding an appropriate tree was a matter of judgment, perseverance, and luck. In that dry, windy country few of the cedars grew straight and full, so the major problem was to find the one least lopsided and wind-whipped. We would drive slowly along the red-dirt roads, peering through the isinglass peepholes of our touring car's side curtains, although some December Sundays would have decent enough weather for us to roll up the curtains and make our inspection directly. There was a mild bit of competition implicit in seeing another carload of people making the same search along the same road. Now and then we would recognize the other family as being friends, and we would combine our efforts.

Another problem in the tree-cutting expeditions was what might be called second-stage. Having found the least-twisted tree up on its hillside, we would stand around and debate (the adults, that is) whether or not it was small enough to be gotten into the house yet full enough to

hide its defects. This thing of tree size was a constant concern of mine. I secretly wished we would some time end up with an enormous green giant and not realize its dimensions until it was too late to do anything about it. I had established a private scale for family prestige based wholly on the size of one's Christmas tree, the bigger the tree the more important the family. It didn't do me much good. We never lived in one of those magnificent homes with fourteen-foot ceilings, therefore the women in the family were very keen about warning my father of the deceptive qualities of cedar trees on hillsides as opposed to cedar trees cut and erected in our living rooms. My father was my ally in wanting a huge tree, but every year we lost our little war and ended up with what I considered no more than a bush that scarcely sustained the modest pile of presents at its feet.

Being the only man in the family (I hardly qualified at the time), my father found himself under constant criticism and direction, not just in choosing a Christmas tree but in every action he took. We lived closely, he, my mother and I, my grandmother and my great-grandmother on my mother's side—and that was the way the grandmothers always lined up: on my mother's side. Although I loved them devotedly, the women of my maternal family were without peer as questioners-after-the-fact. They also had a sort of unconcealed scorn for men and their ways which, while not downright mean, was awfully challenging to a male. They were trained to be doubtful, especially of males. But it was not just men; nothing was ever going to work out right. From young daughter to old granny, they had this bent toward disaster: doomsayers and suspicious of fortune. As for men, these women held that, with few exceptions (mostly dead), they were creatures of weakness, simple lust, and natural ignorance. Especially (as he was the sole example at hand) my father. Once, when I was six years old,

this contest between male and female

domestic forces came perilously close,

despite their strait-laced view of the institu-

tion, to breaking up my parents' marriage.

A too-big Christmas tree was the cause.

My father was a

generous, unstinting man, easygoing and

given to much joking and more talking.

But he wasn't lazy. He would work eigh-

teen hours a day at a job—or twenty to

finish something. He was high-spirited in

his youth, not exactly hot-headed, but

when he lost his temper there was always

plenty left. He was an attractive man in a genial way, and my mother considered him to have a roving eye. He was terribly impetuous and, to hear the women of the family tell it, irresponsible. He was never very good at making money, either. Or keeping it. He was worse at that.

As is often the case, he was married to a woman very nearly his opposite. My mother was cautious at making any decision, often prolonging the decision until it became an agony. She was a careful handler of money and had a burdening sense of responsibility. She had to be given a map to find the humor in a joke, and on top of it all, she was "the baby" of her family. Though the apron strings might stretch, they never broke. Not for her entire life.

My grandmother was even more cautious and fateful than my mother. She was quite artistic and intelligent, but self-educated to a great extent. Like most self-educated persons, she was usually swayed by her own logic. She was loving and warm on a selective basis and, as a child, I got more than my share of her love and attention. In other words, I was her pet . . . the only child in the extended family. A rivalry had grown up around me between father and mother-in-law. My young father thought he was being denied both his child and his wife.

The great-grandmother whom I have mentioned was simply awesome. Born on the Texas frontier when it was rawest and roughest, she was tough in body, mind, and spirit. All the years I knew her, she never changed patterns or habits: she wore her hair in a tight bun, kept two rusty black dresses for public wear, dipped Levi Garrett's snuff, and had church as her only social outlet. There is little need for me to note that her opinions were as firm as her features—and given in a growl that would tame a wolf. Well, she wasn't really *that* formidable, but she tolerated very little nonsense, and nonsense was mainly what young men and boys produced, in her view.

It was a hard time, a crucial time, for my father; young, so young, and burdened not only with wife and child but with two constant critics armed with age and respectability. And he was never sure of his young wife, whose loyalties must have seemed to lie wholly with those old female detractors. He was demonstrative, romantic, passionate. She, although pretty as a girl, had been brought up in the code which considered physical attraction something to be repressed rather than enjoyed. Marriages were made in heaven and not in the bedroom. And to insure an extra measure of uncertainty, my mother and father had married at a tragically young age: she turned sixteen and he twenty the day of their wedding.

But it would be a mistake for me to leave the impression that everything about the marriage and the family was tense and cold. My father was too carefree for that and, as a matter of fact, when one of those four-sided arguments wasn't going on, affairs were delightful among us because they were all four interesting people—my father as a storyteller with my mother as half-willing foil, my grandmother with her poet's flights of beauty when she wasn't looking with fear at the future, and my great-grandmother's historic recollections of her remote girlhood. Only when the lone man faced the three-woman majority did tension and destruction hover over our heads. Then, even I knew it.

The Christmas I have referred to came late in the 1920s. We had driven down the rural roads to the village of Buffalo Gap on our annual tree hunt and had seen nothing from the road that looked to be the right size and shape. One of the older women sniffed and said she knew as much, we had waited too late to go looking—although with millions of cedars available and only about 20,000 people in our town, I don't see how it could have mattered.

We turned off the main road onto a dirt track which was left over from the nineteenth century, called the old Belle Plain wagon road. It led east toward Cedar Gap and passed through the thickest stand of growing cedars. We had moved into a new house (though a small one) and my father declared this was the year to get what he called "a *real* tree." Nobody said anything as we stopped the car, got out and climbed through the barb-wire fence to make a closer inspection of the cedar brakes. True to his declaration, my father went for the big ones, and despite the growing clamor of the women, telling him each tree was unthinkably huge, he managed to cut a full, round beauty which even I could see was going to lift the very roof of our new house.

Too big . . . too big . . . too big!

All three of the women fussed and chorused it over and over. My father defended his choice with some force: "I didn't come from three generations of journeyman carpenters not to be able to gauge how high a tree is!"

The great-grandmother sniffed, "I can tell you one thing . . . you'll never get that 'un in the house."

My grandmother, meanwhile, was shaking

her head and making sad comments con-
cerning the folly of which her son-in-law was
capable because of "that hard-headed streak
in him." And my mother was urging, "Carl
. . . can't you pick another tree? Find one that
makes sense."

My father got tight-lipped and silent—
and in a laugher you know that's a bad
sign. He ceased arguing with them, which
is equally ominous, and began dragging
the big cedar toward the fence. I was the
only one he asked help from (which I
joyously gave) and once through the fence,
we roped that huge growing thing to the
front fender and my father announced to
the world at large (which at the moment

was struggling through the barb-wire fence) that anybody who was planning on riding back to town with him had better grab a root and growl—one of his favorite imperatives. After negotiating the fence without his help, the women settled themselves in the car and, like Birnam Wood removing to Dunsinane, we rolled toward home.

The drive back to town was cooler even than the December afternoon. When we neared the city limits, we joined a caravan of other returning Christmas tree cutters, but there was no comment from our frozen circle about the superior size of *our* green trophy.

As we unloaded the tree, in the civilized confines of residential lots, clipped hedges, and sidewalks, it was evident that our evergreen went beyond the limits of our ceiling—or maybe even our roof. My grandmother broke the long silence: "You'll have to cut it from the top and that will ruin it."

"I will not," my father said, with stolid emphasis.

"Carl," my mother said, "I'd like to know how you think we can use this monster."

"Just wait," he said.

With my help—the women stiffly with-drawn—my father dragged and pushed the tree through the front door and into the living room. One look was sufficient.

"Oh my Lord . . . You'll have to saw it in half."

There was a happy chorus of we-told-you-sos.

"Stay right here," my father shouted. "I'll show you."

He ran toward the kitchen, where he stored his tools, and in a moment came back into the living room with a big, old-fashioned auger he inherited from one of those three generations of journeyman carpenters he had talked about. He knelt down and before the first woman could scream, began boring a hole in the floor.

The uproar broke instants later, and all three of them were on him: awkward, uncoordinated—but effective. He threw down the auger and with a roar of outraged manhood, and fighting clear of the scene of his near-crime, ran from the house. We heard the car start, then the scattering of gravel as he wheeled away.

My mother stood, stricken, looking from the mound of tree to the door and then back at the tree. My grandmother broke into tears and moaned, "He'll not be back . . . not this time."

My great-grandmother, mentioning her own unhappy second marriage, began telling my mother that no man was worth it. And I, for the first time, found myself not the pampered little boy but an isolated male, guilty (for all I knew) of all the vices they were now earnestly ascribing to all men. Alone in a group of sorrowing, aggrieved women, I felt as if it were my fault, both for being masculine and for having secretly prayed for a too-big tree.

Night came on. A half-hearted supper was prepared and tasted, but not eaten. About nine o'clock, my old granny announced she was going home and go to bed, Carl or no Carl. My mother and my grandmother held a halting, whispered conference, then the two older women left for the house they shared a few blocks

44
A. C. Greene

away. My mother noticed me and spoke sharply: "What are you doing up this hour of night?"

"I want to wait for Daddy," I said.

"He's not coming back," she said bitterly, and pushed me off to bed.

It was a kind of growing up, that time I lay there in my bed, in the dark, wondering and fearing at what had happened. My parents, who had always been mother and daddy suddenly were other people, neither Mother nor Daddy, but two individuals—strangers to whom I, for the first time in my little life, was not the primary consideration. I went to sleep as confused as I was afraid.

But he did come back. It was after midnight when he knocked on the front door and my mother, in her robe, went to find him there. She said he was grinning and holding one of the ridiculous sort of gifts he was always coming up with: a carton of packaged peanuts he had found in the middle of a boulevard.

I woke when I heard hammering and movement in the living room, but for a while I lay in the dark, uncertain what was happening. The noises stopped and I could hear my father talking, then there was no more conversation.

I got out of bed quietly and slipped to the living room door and peeked in. My mother and father, looking so young that even I was struck by it, were sitting on a rug in the middle of the floor, holding each other tightly and shedding the kind of tears I sensed were from happiness, not sorrow. They were gazing at the Christmas tree which took up one entire end of the room and was pushed into a ninety-degree bend against the ceiling a yard or so from its tip.

And that is still my idea of Christmas.

Christmas Shopping

A Reminiscence

was just seven years old, my first Christmas shopping trip. I had started to school that past September and felt very grown up. I went on the shopping trip with my Grandmother Cole, who was our city's Carnegie librarian and worked downtown and was, therefore, a citizen of that mysterious adult world which "went to work" every morning instead of making up beds and washing dishes and ironing clothes the way my mother did. My grandmother took me Christmas shopping on Saturday, not because she had the day off but because I did. She had to be away from her job, and she got a day's pay deducted, too. This was during the Great Depression, so giving up a day's pay was a serious and substantial matter.

To buy gifts, I was equipped with twenty-five cents which I was to carry in a mitten. I hated mittens, but my mother insisted I wear them because (she said) I wasn't old enough for gloves. I suspect the truth was, she couldn't afford to buy me a pair of gloves so long as my childish mittens were wearable.

My grandmother and I set out early

from the house we lived in on the south
edge of our West Texas town. We didn't
have to worry about waiting for the stores
to open. In those days they opened at
8 A.M. We had to walk several blocks to the
Fair Park to catch the streetcar, which
made a loop at that point and returned to
the downtown district.

That Saturday morning was bright but
chilly and, as I remember, it was the end of
the second week in December. Later—
years later—when I was in business for
myself, I prayed for cold, sloppy weather
during the Christmas buying season because it seemed to inspire the customers
to spend money. In fact, an old, wise

merchant had told me, the first year I owned a store, that I should hope for bad weather the day after Thanksgiving because that started the buying season off right.

"They *shop* when the weather's pretty—they *buy* when the weather's cold," he said. I believed him. I still have my store ledger, and on those Yuletide days when it was drizzly or mushy or cloudy, I have so noted on that day's page with a great deal of underlining and exclamation points ("Sleet!!!" "SNOW!?!") and a proud arrow drawn to the sales total at the foot of the page.

But returning to the 1930s: my grandmother and I boarded the little four-wheel trolley on the Fair Park loop—the men who were waiting all tipping their hats and letting the women and children on first. Pretty soon we were bumping and swaying up Sayles Hill on our way to downtown. The ride seemed extremely lengthy and adventuresome to me, although it couldn't have been that drawn-out, even by dinky trolley: the entire streetcar system of our town was barely five miles long.

We bumped our way east on South Seventh Street, turned down Chestnut

Street, bumped even more bouncily over the railroad tracks, and suddenly were on Pine, the main street, impatiently clanging through a crowd of Model T Fords, Reo Flying Clouds, Whippets, and pedestrians along the decorated downtown avenues. "You may push the buzzer," my grandmother informed me, and I was thrilled almost to the point of terror. Pushing the buzzer on the streetcar was definitely a grownup's job. You simply could not trust a youngster to do it. In his excitement he would always push it too soon, at the wrong corner, or keep pushing it so long that it made a continual buzzing noise which annoyed the motorman.

I had to stand in the woven-wicker seat to reach the buzzer, which was mounted halfway up the window frame. I looked around to see if some adult was going to push it before I could, but one of the men passengers smiled at me and said, "Go ahead, son. You buzz for all of us." When the time came I hit it just right. The trolley car squealed to a hissing halt right at the corner of Pine and North First, depositing us in the middle of the street. I noticed that half a dozen others got off at the same stop and was quite proud to know that I, alone, had halted this magnificent vehicle.

"First we will go to the bank," my grandmother announced, taking my hand.

This embarrassed me, to some degree—her taking my hand—although I expected it to happen. My grandmother was a most cautious woman and wouldn't think of letting a seven-year-old, even her favorite grandson, walk, detached, across the hurly-burly of downtown traffic. To her credit, she did release my hand as soon as we reached the sidewalk. I solved the problem, later, by pretending to take *her* arm and escorting *her* through the crush of Model T's. The traffic lights had bells on them which rang merrily every time the signal changed, and my grandmother warned me not to ever try to start across a downtown street until the bell finished ringing.

*B*anks were open on

Saturdays, in those days—if they were

open at all. The Depression had closed a

good many, even in smaller towns like

ours that had once supported three or four

banks. We walked into the marble magnifi-

cence of the Farmers & Merchants Bank,

with one of the officers speaking politely

to my grandmother and a departing cus-

tomer (male) tipping his hat as he held the

door for us to enter the lobby. My Grand-

mother Cole was not a woman of sub-

stance, but as the city's librarian, she was

well known and esteemed.

Going to a teller's cage, she transacted

her business, using her passbook and get-

ting a deposit credit from the teller, who

wore a green eyeshade and black sleeve

protectors, and wrote with pen and ink. As

we left the bank, other men bowed or

tipped their hats (all the men wore hats in

those days and I, too, had on a cloth cap)

or spoke agreeably, which made me quite

proud to have such a grandmother—and

quite possibly eroded a bit of the parental

respect I should have had for my father,

poor man who at that particular period

found himself not only without the bank-

ers' respect but without a job.

"Shall we look in at Minter's Dry Goods?"

my grandmother asked me. Feeling, to

make sure the quarter was still in my mitten, I agreed. We entered Minter's and I
was hit by a wave of that lovely old mer-
cantile smell which disappeared sometime
after World War II—a combination of the
odor of red floor sweep, crisp cotton cloth
off the bolt, perfume or face powder some
woman might be sampling, and an unde-
finable feminine odor which haunted me
to the point of uneasiness, a boy intruding
into this woman's world.

I chose a little white handkerchief with
a red rose embroidered in one corner for
Granny—which was the name by which I
called my great-grandmother. I handed my
grandmother my quarter, she handed it to

the saleslady, the saleslady wrote some-

thing on her sales slip, put everything in a

small, round leather container, screwed the

container onto an overhead receptacle,

jerked a wooden handle—and the recep-

tacle shot off up to the cashier on a tight,

singing wire. These wires ran from the

cashier's cage on the balcony to every part

of the store. Every store of any magnitude

at all had this overhead trolley system. In a

moment, back down the wire would come

the receptacle to the saleslady; she would

unscrew the leather holder, shake out your

purchase slip and your change, hand it all

to you, along with your package, smile and

say, "Thank you, come back to see us,"

and (especially if the clerk happened to be a man) wink at me.

We repeated the process at Grissom's, Mims, and Campbell's Dry Goods. I have forgotten, I hate to admit, what I bought for my mother and father or my other grandmother, but I do recollect asking my Grandmother Cole if I had enough left out of my quarter to buy Uncle a present. Uncle was her only son and my favorite kinsman. She looked in her purse and said I had just enough, if I chose carefully. I got him a little lacquer box to hold small matches. Uncle, despite my pious family's concern for his health and his morals, smoked cigarettes.

$\mathscr{A}$t lunchtime we stood in line outside The Cave, a popular basement restaurant, and waited to get a table. Men who came out of the restaurant, having finished their meal, never failed to speak or raise their hats to my grandmother. The women, especially those her age, would make some little tender gesture to me and remark on my bright eyes, or my red hair, or something other than my robustness, because I was skinny as a rail and there was absolutely no room for compliments there. Two or three of the younger women asked about my mother, "Don't tell me Marie's got the flu?" or something ominous (to my ears) like that. The truth was, as I learned years later, my mother was so humiliated that her young husband was out of work that she wouldn't be seen doing Christmas shopping with her mother. "They'd know very well where the money was coming from—my own mother, and a widow to boot," she sobbed.

In front of the Farmers & Merchants Bank and the Citizens National Bank stood Salvation Army lassies with their kettles and their hand bells, ringing and ringing. I hesitantly dropped two cents in one kettle, trying to cover up the paucity of my offering, but the Salvation Army lady pretended it was a dollar bill, saying, "Oh, thank you, honey," to me. (Santa Clauses didn't man the Christmas kettles in our town until several years later.)

The McLellan Variety Store had two fascinating machines at work: one was a popcorn popper which stood near the sidewalk as you entered the north door, the other was a doughnut-making machine located just inside the east door. The popcorn machine had little mechanical men who appeared to do the work, turning cranks and bending over to empty the full basket when the corn had popped. The doughnut machine sent a delicious sugary fragrance all over the store and also formed an exhibit, with the ovals of dough

sliding up and around from the automatic cutter, to fall into the cooking oil then be propelled, one at a time, out onto a screen to be served. We bought a sack of popcorn for a nickel but decided we couldn't afford another nickel for two doughnuts. I got to carry the popcorn sack and, of course, ate practically all the popcorn. My grand- mother was very dignified, as befit a Carnegie librarian, and was careful of her actions in public. It was not seemly for a woman of her age and stature to be seen marching along munching on buttered popcorn, especially carrying the sack.

Once, as we were shopping on Cypress Street, which was slightly more elegant than Pine, the fire trucks came screaming right by us from the Central Fire Station, heading toward some conflagration and I was ready to dance from excitement, but my grandmother warned me against displaying too much joy at the passage of the fire trucks. "It could mean that some other little boy won't have a very nice Christmas, if his house is on fire," she pointed out. I tried to suppress my fascination but couldn't wrench my eyes away from the red engines until they disappeared. "I hope it's just a false alarm," I said, a touch too sanctimoniously to be convincing. In my seven-year-old mind I could see flames shooting out in all directions from some big two-story house. With the occupants standing safe in the front yard, to be sure.

Then, as the December shadows began drawing 'round, we boarded the streetcar at the stop in front of the Woolworth store and headed home. The day had grown overcast and the car was stuffed with shoppers and their packages, but we were all tired and didn't do much talking. My grandmother and I were immediately offered a seat by two men when we boarded the loaded trolley. I was so weary I didn't even

resent the fact that I didn't get to push the buzzer, because our stop was at the end of the line so the car came to a halt without my help.

As we descended from the trolley, the air pump going "thump-thump-tonk" under the floorboards, and the motorman yelling, "'Bye, ever'body!" it started to snow. Just the lightest kind of a downy flake, but real snow for West Texas at Christmas time. It was a rare miracle and it made the day perfect.

We walked joyously through the snow to our home, and as we were setting down our packages on the dining room table my grandmother held out a dime and said,

"Here is the change from your quarter."

Dear lovely soul. Of course, there had been no change, even in those days when a quarter bought a full meal. No change? Why, she had spent hard earned and scarce money of her own buying my gifts, letting me think my quarter was more than covering all the purchases. I think I must have had some sense of this because I hesitated, holding the dime in my palm (no mitten). But I kept it . . . how could a seven-year-old expect to feel guilt or concern over a gift dime, even in hard times?

A wonderful experience, a distant, silvery memory to me now: my first Christmas shopping trip. And, bless her sweet shade, wherever in paradise it abides, it occurred to me only on Christmas morning as our family was opening the gift packages, who the one person was for whom I had forgotten to buy a present.

The End